Kelptown

Also by Carol Watts

When Blue Light Falls (Shearsman Books, 2018)
Dockfield (Equipage, 2017)
56, a poem sequence (with George Szirtes, Arc Publications, 2016)
Many Weathers Wildly Comes (Spiralbound/Susakpress, 2015)
Flete, artist's book (2014)
Sundog (Veer Books, 2013)
Mother Blake (Equipage, 2012)
Occasionals (Reality Street Editions, 2011)
this is red (Torque Press, 2009)
Wrack (Reality Street Editions, 2007)
brass, running (Equipage, 2006)
alphabetise, artist's book (2005)

Carol Watts

Kelptown

Shearsman Books

First published in the United Kingdom in 2020 by
Shearsman Books Ltd
PO Box 4239
Swindon
SN3 9FN

Shearsman Books Ltd Registered Office
30–31 St. James Place, Mangotsfield, Bristol BS16 9JB
(this address not for correspondence)

www.shearsman.com

ISBN 978-1-84861-733-9

Acknowledgments

Some of the poetry from this collection has been previously published in *Cordite Poetry Review, Datableed, Dusie, electric wood spectra, The Goose, Tentacular, This Corner* and *Truck magazine*. I've included acknowledgements and other connected materials in the notes. Heartfelt thanks to all the editors.

Particular warm thanks are due to friends: Lisa Samuels, for the kauris that made me see my own shores; Dave Maric, for our collaboration in 2016 which resulted in his work, *Vigil*; and especially Will Montgomery, for what has been a transformative exchange in making work over a number of years, and for reminding me of Marianne Moore's 'The Fish' as I moved to Brighton's Kemptown.

Cover image: Spinach leaf as scaffolding for beating heart cells.
With permission and thanks to Professor Glenn Gaudette of Worcester Polytechnic Institute, USA.

Contents

Kelptown

Life Scores

Notes on a Burning World

DeExtinction Poems

For my sisters, with love

Kelptown

You ask me whom the *Macrocystis* alga hugs in its arms?
Study, study it, at a certain hour, in a certain sea I know.

Pablo Neruda

Kelptown

1

Slippery condominium, finding a foothold perilous
to a resting here, each green cell an inhabiting,
each morning a remaking of us.

How do I live, tenant amongst your long fronds.
Gathering the means to remain, my glutinous
high rise swaying, extending northward.

I saw you southern among islands, your forests
great and hospitable. Subterranean bark mimicking
striated skin of whales, breaching kauris

reverenced in terrestrial reserve, as if balance
could be struck and mean more than fortune,
more than my shaven head and a chance wind.

I saw you in a western bay, spreading sugar
under sea planes and container ships, so refuge
lay in invited anthropologies of relation

that might give me entry. None but
fantasies of attachment ballooning new galls
from my limbs as if to compensate, made

to become my own vacant property, as if
a keening of orcas might echo more resonant
from basements and kitchenettes, my studio

compression. Your real estate. So here I am
renting vegetal architecture, my body
failing in form, perverse and vainly adaptive.

I am seeking you, unsuitable for attachment.
Distribution is sporadic, but here is a home
on friable shores, built from inundate truths.

Made and remade, no stone to grip without rolling,
depositional and uncertain, no holdfast place,
yet we live here, and daily discover this.

2

Unkempt we are. Sea hours catch us
waiting, while cat-sharks strew purses
more distantly, as if you might find

poor returns scattered in the street.
Keep your eyes down and scan for reward.
Watch them born again, repeatedly, marine.

The way the word unnamed became unarmed.
The way a blow to the head became a blow
to the heart, how cruelty warps the tongue.

Yet the forest grows up and us woven in it,
already fathoms down and singing cellular
where the ground once was, and our words

for world migrating. Our streets rise up,
like ribbons, oar-weed, rooted tangle.
Suddenly walking the vertical, finding

ourselves swimming in uncertain light,
gills breaking out, to adapt, if only to adapt
without knowing what will right us

without surface or air. Caught waiting
in the doorway, he was shoeless.
I am embarrassed, he said, looking down,

the way pavement normalizes as home,
as if a shoeless state would be no more than
to tread softly and then their sudden

disappearance. As if all living devastations
are rendered domestic in safe evolution,
the next pair mutating to flip-flops

and then to bloodied feet. Kicking water.
Still he waits while the hours gather,
those bright bubbles collecting underside.

3

Fleshy feet lost on the lee, to the receding
tide, sounding at night. The absence of footfall
and the screaming birds, their wider surround

given up until a rousing. But here, so much deeper,
the long chains sway, barely moving in the midst
of storms and currents, or in the paths of predatory

arrivals, thickets marginalia from a childhood
fable, thornless and accommodating. I can hear
the scrabbling of limbs above, the wash in

frequencies, informatic tones. Or venturing out
ahead of anticipated dramas, rapid explosions
of encounter, I drag my carapace along

for possible exit, that game of covering the eyes
ingrained and delusional. *So is it you here, hen*?
Working your economy, without touching mine.

Eddying past bondage wear, plastic buckets,
ladders and seaside gelateria, the blooming neon,
a florescence of night pharmacies provoking fury,

this plying of energy and survival meets
in the sea's measure, like we might all become
supple as seals rather than rock-beached

angry as we are, and make from this rush
a shelter, by some form of caddis principle, husk
become home. To indicate a hope in metamorphosis

glued to our living, and buoyed up. Bladderless,
but constructing subterranean housings, that
change might happen in more than dreams.

Pure biofuel we become. Mucilaginous thrust,
resisting direction, capture; firing imaginary
will, somehow holds out beautiful making, still.

4

Held to place, unknowing. Or by a bruise,
as darkening conduct under skin, showing up
in small capillaries past impact sparking

a fretwork in red lines. Attachment building
from hurt, maybe pain, at that point where
you think: some *thing* happened here, can't bring it

to mind, was it collision, or did it bloom social
from beneath. Deeper disorders manifest,
inevitable constancies just waiting to be read.

A system of ties, and the way the body shows
its metre unbidden. I woke up with bruises.
Did you see that happening, or is it broken

auto-immunity painting out its plaint
as if sleepwalking and nothing to show
but sodden feet, and briny pathways

dripping over thresholds, my own ghost,
now guessing at a haunted lifeline
turned golden green, black as sunflowers,

waxy as that Victorian show on a beach front.
See what happens to organs where pleasure
goes coastal wild, how we all suffer!

What house is this now, raising glutinous
heights? It has grown here so long chained
to uncertain holdfast, with tools ranged in

intent, rusting saw, painted horse,
scaffolding and underlay, balconies refusing
gentrification in the rain. She came up

flaring outrage. *How would you like it*
if this was YOU, with HER doing that
in your street? Answer me.

5

Listen to rivers and levels, hefting where
fog rolls over, the undead are at home for local
apocalypse among the silent sheep, sheen of

distant metallic seas. What is it to find this land
removed, and with it a secure measure of tilt.
Mass and contour. *How would you like it,*

she said, if you woke one day and found yourself
tethered to the vertical, barely able to hold your
breath, and endless drownings arriving oceanic,

oxygen coming through the pores, and that too
rare to speak on the miracle of submergence?
Street commotion a reminder of a lost world

I don't need reminding of. Where we built so
carefully, unthinking, because our future tends
to a beckoning, as it tilts. Stripping out cellulose

that keeps all upright, taking on transfusions.
Suddenly this watery home began to beat.
A green heart, pushing out aortic, growing

like a heart from a leaf, its vascular intention
transparent as the entrails of a shrimp, seeded
with human living. Red capillaries spreading

through excavated green, really, is this us
now discovering substitutions, or growing new
organs as we may, our house throbbing with

accommodation. Rivers of us return on a king tide,
rehoused and newly made. Or this heart redundant
for another living, spawning from habituation.

So time is cellular traversal, and love with it,
unbound, marshalling local memories,
learning as we move, or finding a beat.

6

That it could rest us here, futures all aligned.
That we could trust to calmer currents, knowing
I might leave and yet care for you still, this world

rolling through, beneath squalls and ghost nets,
entanglement sprayed into galaxies, moon tides,
the swell eating into balance, as it has always done,

lit by pulsing lanterns, ballooning and delicate,
larger than human, sieving their delicate organzas,
long electric trails stinging signs into amnesia.

I have forgotten what was possible, since you left.
The future is noisy in insistence, and yet silent.
At night the trails of phosphorous, pulse.

Imagined land without meadows, as it was,
already broken to margins you did not recognize
as a child, *how do I move, there*? What *is* that?

Now deep and submarine, rusting growth
engines, hulks blooming chemical gardens, slow
to return, tenanted anemones might snatch granular

prospects, interrupted genomes, drawing from
damage to discover affordances, bee masks,
deextinction a combination of small wills

ravenous to maintain themselves in undoing.
Animals continue seeding the future, some
evolve without a mouth to eat, do the dance

while they are warm to it, no need any more
for this mouthing, this pathfinding, this
fusion of tongue and feeling, you'd think

living is all now beyond words. Yes we find in
simplicity and roaring the defence of meadows,
smaller insects, what is common in this. *Explain.*

Hammerheads

Ah – the sea!
Emily Dickinson

The sea grows old in it.
Marianne Moore

1

Found, unkempt
        among higher tides, that

hulk listing over arches.

The sea rose, with its angers,
leaving us to gaze upward, to air,

the massing of hammerheads.
Float glaucous light, holding

to crevices against the current.
Edge town, rusting

in sight, subterranean.

How they gather, blunt and flicking
above us,
        the drunken singing.

2

There was a hurling of limbs.

That first day, hatchet vision
          took in the pier, the excision of light

disaggregating.

Seeing much of what is behind us.

Sensitive to electric fields. That winter glare
          picks up cleanly, magenta pink

                                        base corals.

Already blasted, so furious in his detaching, the steel
          crushes, legless.

The way vision has to sweep in predatory ways.

The way it has to, to maintain a holding space

or hover blindly.

3

Already the sea has been here, and left the downs

                    a chalky banking up of husks
and bodies, skeletal wave
                                        flats.

Returns as imagined volume in the street, such depth!

As transparency, and sleeping bodies

            turning, as if wrasse will gather for them, even in
                        open mouths, strip falsely, managing

coastal erosion in the doorway.

No hold to shelter in, but that velvety blue illusion of
                        lunglessness, of adaptation to poor

exposure, in these pale bleachings, older
                                shafts of daylight.

4

All the marks are here to read by.

They would tell us how we got here
        facing out, the whitest of facings.

Somewhere invisible is France, beyond the rotors of wind farms,
        container ships, under the waters
                                        brown, sometimes lilac

        gilding, the white fringes.

There are evenings from this first floor window when

        hammerheads meet me with that eddying gait, eye to eye,

        the way they sweep in detection, getting on with naysaying.

The point of gathering is swimming this continental shelf, redrawing it.

I think of them as domestic but they are much wilder, in truth they
        retain that.

I identify with their schooling.

Home of fumeroles, of hammerheads
        and in season, the kelp forests, tall as the water once was.

5

Hammerheads are inadvertent hosts, their accommodation
blind spots, pinioned north of the head.

Gentler populations hang out in increasing shoals there.

It would seem a hovering and distribution, that bourgeois split
between blind safety and predatory drives.

And yet they look to gather in their sleekness.

And yet we look to gather.

Nonetheless vulnerable to.

What is watching from above.

Who sees that elastic curve, this hammerhead community

writ into cartilage, the beauty of non-Euclidean promise

shot through some pelvic hook.

In the end, a simple flickery of bodies in real time.

Echo sounding, when sight fails.

6

Once the impossibility of slopes clothed with fish, the valleys standing so thick.

That they shall.

Flocks of vestige.

Safely graze.

Settle the runnels, the morays and the teeth.

Woolly shoals.

The noise of the seas.

You imagine domination through remnants, and then see it everywhere, insistently in pieces.

It replaces synapses, shorting across the gaps, that's how dangerous.

The swell which took us, has already taken us.

7

On those days when hammerheads are absent

as when crowds empty out

the detritus of gathering recomposing emptiness

as when wind picks up and the sea churns edgily

you can see the earth is moving and this a margin

on those days to sit is to enter that reverie

    which sits as salt flats do, cracked and fissile

uninhabited   where air is suddenly humid

    outsourcing some warm tone of living

I think do I wait for their return

    the sheen of their patience mirroring among them

    the carriage of this extraction of hours

8

Did I wake with you this morning?

Your long grey iridescent flank somehow dulled in light.

The sea stops tumbling in the shallows.

And all the jewels, their wet glossiness, the sheen, lost
to the edge of day, turn towards dryness.

I wonder will this air extract life, a reverse vacuum
driving out the capacity of seas, your gills

working doubletime to retain it.

The smoothness of stones, their lithic properties, returned
in denial of water.

Caught in your skin, its impermeable teeth, its hidden
helix binding you to possible future movement.

Or to the stasis of sleep, the way you hang there.

9

Did I wake this morning and find you gone?

Hammerhead you have the widest of visions, could see already
the shape of vacating, that print

                    in the bed as imagined presence, as a cast of you.

And then we all gather for travelling, remembering that imprint, the time
it was made and the life that filled it.

I packed it like a bell.

Ringing under the ocean for my inundated town.

Calling us in.

Did I wake this morning, unsealing this.

Species dream.

10

How that dream went on a journey!

It was a drover, it pushed along my lanes past the rippling of grasses,
watery transhumance might lead me further.

It bleached all the corals so I could see the definition of the lived.

Yet that definition was not where I thought, something had broken down.

My heart had already started bleaching, so I did not recognize where
I began or ended.

My fingers were brittle, snapping for ornament.

Camouflage is exquisitely wrought.

Those who can, do it.

How white I became, among the cliffs and facings of white.

Shoring up in dreamwork.

This internal calcifying, as if buying time for equivalences.

My heart, a death of a million creatures.

My heart, this reef.

Valediction, for the Loves of Barnacles

Out on the currents now, reached along as far
as the warmth breeds us, and shacked up.
Nothing to do but spawn as we are sucked in
to bilgewater warnings, and then spewed up
on jetties, which is to say the length of, where
you pass by. You did not think of me as a delicacy
but I was, building long white sheaths. Let me
grow geese, the long necks become other than I
will have been, and take flight.

Herons are too large for the trees today, scale
offends. Geese accrete, own intent in migrations.
Find advantage of regularity in neighbourliness,
sky formations. Fly over at five o'clock daily
with all that carping, set off from Iceland after
grazing. Engines beat, hollow. Will is fuelled up
then it ends. Releases in landing. You do not
have the worry of winter heating, she said. Let me
stop, holding the bars.

Calcic thing. Glut of tidemarks extinguished by
rising, crust of anchors around sounds said in
built up tenderness. Pressed down in hurt, pale
calluses picked away at. Where we come together
walls are removed in soft economies. Your voice
reassures more than your presence. O colonies
fill the gaps in the floor where the water rises,
said as an afterthought. It is your fault so you must
help. Nothing will grow.

The king tide is lusty about us. It swells
for the time it does, we emerge more freshly
than nations. Exposed, in multiples, closing
small beaks. Internal features only venture
out on its passing, the lightest extension.
A brush of pine branches in silent woods.
The plume of a seed which must fall to
the ground, the fringed leg of a boatman,
questions of air and water.

Fear of resemblances in this love of catastrophe.
Harm holds repositories for election. Are you.
Culled and cut down, scraped out in sluices
and motors. Where the knife drags over surfaces
with some interference, then finds its way between.
Reefs also cut but they are not the same. What
is the same in variation. Carry unspoken letters
to mend the damage, for times of disturbance.
This remainder, eyes.

What was it you liked in these instances of.
Encounter, without ceremony or marking.
The most beautiful, curved, prehensile teeth
and tremulous hands. Charles Bronson in the
cheap seats reluctantly. The chance of a clear sky.
To offer nothing beyond the excavation of rocks,
and their undulations, until being prised away.
Or was it shelter, the way I might share my coat
with you in the dark, rain.

At night the tide is low. Haunted by imagined
radios regarded as testimony. Or crackle of a
singing voice. I will find you when you are gone.
What remains after. The breeze is unrelenting

with windows on both sides, sucking. Curtains
out, flapping quietly. Listen. Nothing else moves
freely. In this world without, the ascendancy of
other. I am held to where I am in later stages by
a making.

Under such calciferous trees. Living is sifted
through the teeth, gathered and thrusted. Fat
with absorbance, or bone thin. In endless growth,
we diminish remorselessly. Will water rise now
without anchorage for settlement. I hear words
in an updraft, hoping they are spoken. I will
sieve them as whales manage, when their ribs
show through. Be human, he said today, and not
yourself.

A dream that offspring will always remain
in his house. Those summers sitting on the deck,
while his name rests among them without
words. The hill still rising over red roofs.
Now we change sex at will, are grown in gelatin.
What is it that shields us and our loose wandering.
In his eyes, is there disappointment. Clap that rhythm,
no one of us is what we thought. Anticipate nothing
more than the beating of it.

Sea Life, or Kropotkin's Tank

Perhaps it was a space where force suspended.
We might gather and right ourselves for an instant.
It takes a lifetime to acknowledge soft-shelled need,
our skin weathering time as equivalence.
How many seasons pass in finding our feet.
Years leach out saturate hours, glaciers decline.
Now the most familiar estranges, pricked
tension of a sunlit day, heat passing for anxiety
where tideflats reveal us. Waking today to
gentler currents, all those evacuations of living
never captured but plain to sight through this
dull vitrine, care steps in without adrenalin.
Here let me hold my breath enough to find you
while the tide holds off, it warms, we breathe.

All these labours flush inkily, our failures
sweet, purple, blooming in cloud recollection
to afford a getaway, so many years in building,
yet here we are, you and I, in blind making.
Who knows where we are going. Scale opens
inestimable jaws, fear mimicry hounds us,
we push to make contact with the ground.
Take my arm, if we gather & overturn wildly.
Where the squall breaks, unintended news is
contrary to prediction. Where memory recedes
we repeat it by way of retrieval, yet it was
never measure of each day. Tides are captured
in this tank by artificial swell, the physics of being
here no more than rhythm, in watery interleaving.

Duration, exception. Outside a whipping up
of familiar wilds. When Kropotkin came
watching, hours passed, one stood sentinel.
Beyond the sentimental vines, the circulation
of rescue videos, the making of *forever homes*,
domestic entreaties. Net entanglements.
He was impressed by this watchfulness in
mutual aid. Where Fortuna lurches, sideways,
I move the world erratically, yet over time
this path smooths out, such fakery in deliberate
equilibrium! finding solidarities in the righting of
catastrophe. *Stay safe* she said, her shaven head
clear of your grip, so molten in the politics
of the sea, riding out a universal freeloading.

Be like the sea! she said. Kelp is a prairie,
it drops its leaves deciduous, prefers light,
holds off from turbidity, the noise of crowds.
In heat the seagrasses grow brown. Suddenly
overrun, even the deeper forests silence
themselves, multitudinous in migration.
I would find that place to regroup, where we
can begin to renew, or put down conditions.
Taking a stand, fending off this extraction
where currents move too fast for mutual life,
find roots in change. This coast poses mortally,
and you say *I won't be around to see this.*
Yet we move without anchoring, flushed
in the luxury of having already lived enough.

Flushed in the shame of that, pooling
colourful encrusted starfish, this granted
nature of living with all in its place, abdicated
like a linen drawer, domestic, imaginary
inheritances; what it means to assume election,
against the horror of being without, keeping life
on the tab or ekeing out, assured there will be
more where that came from, insistence of
perfection in existing in the tank, as long
as you remain here, the glassy walls, reflection
picking up the greener sheen. Water can shift
like crystal, it arcs, or finds pathways; in truth
you see it contained, not as the force it is, not
the space of manifest forests, of continents.

Life Scores

Good Life Redact # 1

The truth was
hardy
to dive from.
the
puttering of gifts
and counter-gifts
passed
too
quickly.

Our days,
fled from my face.
leisureliness,
came
back in force.

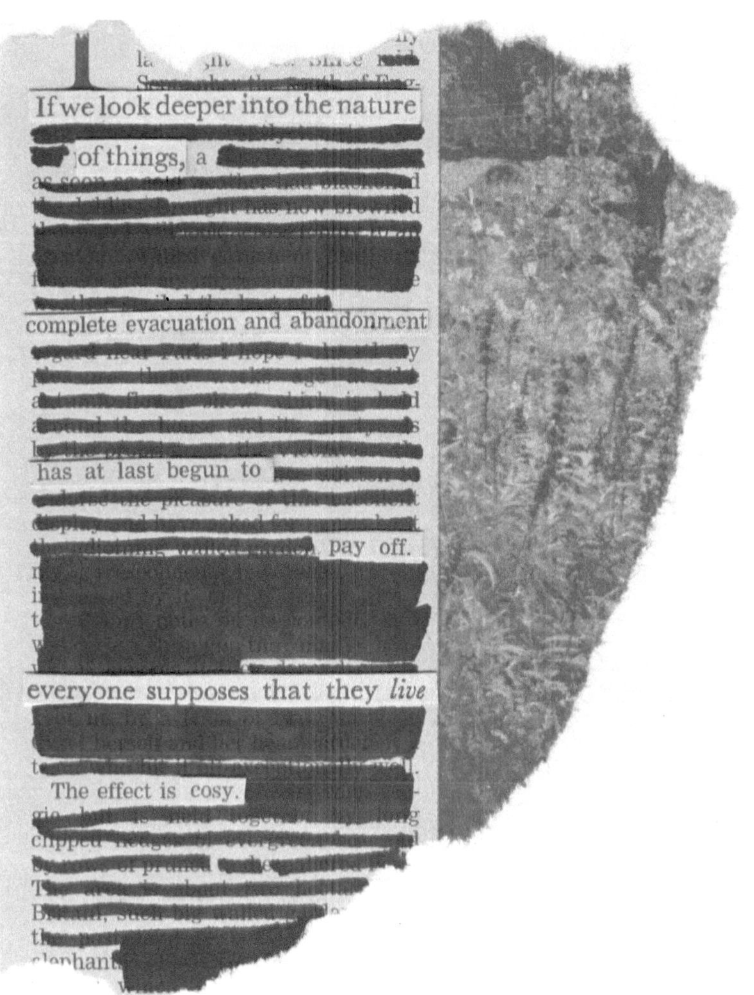
If we look deeper into the nature
of things, a
complete evacuation and abandonment
has at last begun to
pay off.
everyone supposes that they *live*
The effect is cosy.

You either walk along
their back-breaking work whence
and whither
saying
'Enough is *my* misfortune'
Guide price: £3,250,000

Once a week
stubbornly refuse
our immediate
tasteless
custom-made
surroundings
with little more
than a crowbar
and muscle.

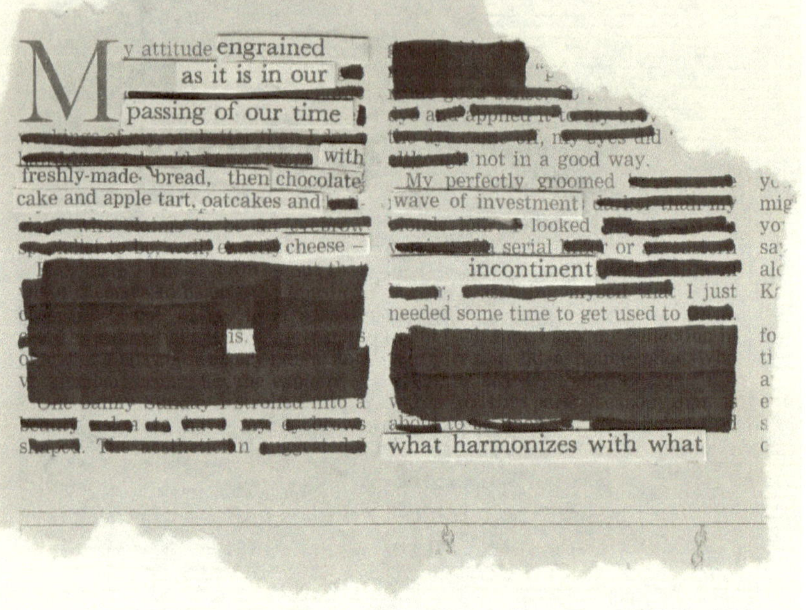

Users' guide:

My attitude engrained
as it is in our
passing of our time
with
freshly-made bread, then chocolate
cake and apple tart, oatcakes and
cheese –
is.

not in a good way.
My perfectly groomed
wave of investment
looked
a serial or
incontinent
, I just
needed some time to get used to
what harmonizes with what

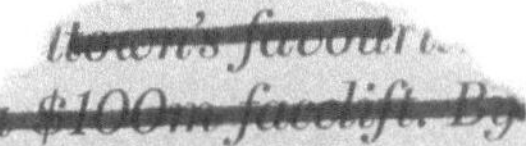
~~town's favouri~~
~~a $100m facelift. By~~

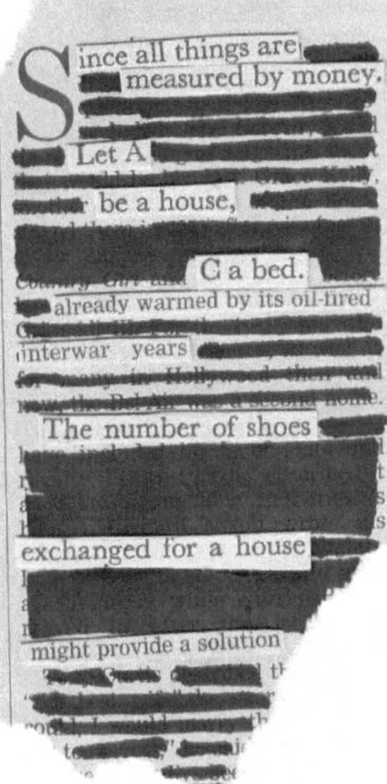
Since all things are
measured by money.
Let A
be a house,
C a bed.
already warmed by its oil-fired
interwar years
The number of shoes
exchanged for a house
might provide a solution

"slowly but surely"
for nice calculation is
a niggardly thing.

But
(*a*), since we
use the word
'know'
for instance,
as people do in
straightening
sticks that are bent.
yeah."
happiness is
*in*complete).

from Brickworks/Vigil

Turbofolk

history gathers like running water
all the stories running through your hands
a coldness in all that trickling motion
the way your skin tries to meet its drowning
the way that words choke with inundation   say:

                    justice   not
                                        a time of justice

always the celebration of defeat
all the loved floating in the Una
snag yes snagging on the shame
how hate is tar   catching on the rocks
you'd think to overcome it
find humanity in unexpected places   yet
the river rolls like money   rolling all before it

                    and its trophies
                                        don't settle

as if you could imagine
all the town dancing
as an occupation of life

as if they came together
in the times of seasons
refusing borders

as if you'd play this
Balkan story
in the interests of love

as if he was never on
the train   where hate
burnt off the day

so the water courses under the brick
you make the brick from fire and clay   and you play it out
so the heat still burns and the city rises
over ruins and waterways   know this   know this
skulls are lighter in their passage   they roll and gather
they are smooth and polished in the rolling
heads banking on financial districts and meeting places
beached under transport hubs and high rises
orderly   among currents   how they move like crowds
as by subterranean festival

justice   in a time of skulls
their language doesn't come easy   do you   you do you

hear them

did he build his house   above water

so it ends.

T.R.E.E. (Total Rare Earth Elements)

A text score for vocal performance originally generated through pencil drawings of wood from a cold shore, the latter now an artist's book.

Prompted by a phrase from Jackson Mac Low's 'It is a Simple Life', and in collaboration with processed field recordings of tree creaks made by sound artist Will Montgomery.

inoculate me

1

rare e arth
rare   rth
r   air earth

It is a simple life under the sun all day without decent water to drink or to wash in / but I never had a sister / the nature of daily life and the coming on is not dramatic / what would a mother do / and yet you do not take it in / what is the occasion for / and rain coming on / I had no advantage in this timing / this timing / without pointing to it before / as much death as anyone could handle / its musculature / taking a skinful and it would not / take / our growing immunity is of the wrong kind / perhaps you did not take it in / she said /

2

washed up / I was washed up on this / shingle / what perfect information / where / but I see you / nothing is invented / in neural pathways / I am queasy and emotional / what is redundant about a way forward / without decent water to drink or to wash in / is it actively managed / he's here / how do you know / what is on my plate / the cycle is almost complete / my father was too young / this is not happening exactly / us / you've been trained well / April / held together by / rare earth magnets / damaged a digestive tract / gradually I grow / darker / I can offer few examples / letters obtrude / there is no need to change / I have many sisters but no mother / what would she / think / it spread so fast / her scalp was alive with it / take it in / she said you do not take it / in /

3

small inhalings / would have protected for centuries / without surgical intervention / this daily life / inter / venes / the hawk adjusts / the marshes were rank close by / but there was clarity / it is too late for / me / words have talked their way / so superficial when / such violence / obtains / I think what is next / where do I / walk / what jetty extends / silence / no do I walk / this jetty / because something / will / follow / I / take it in to myself / this jetty is / on my tongue / is / my tongue / I hurried elsewhere yet / what was in my bones / repeated close to the skull / look look / a pale light / I was born into this / uh - o uh – o / I do regret not seeing you / while you knew / asking / what a move / I must learn to 'take it in' /

4

I'm scared to ask / if you are just going / to / interrupt / there goes angel! / and my jetty / runs out from the shore / sunshine / let me choose to live / and roar / in leaf spoil / sunshine wins / sound of crying birds / it took tremendous fortitude / to survive this / elimination bout / we leave tomorrow / and off it goes / coffee in the sun / I will walk the marsh / one more instance of / regret / without paragraphs / syllabic / procedures / and groups of other women / look look / I am / one / among bones / the world isn't an equal place / it is a simple life / disappeared and working / at that time / what delivers disembarks / at last / pieced / where I am in rewarded / my tongue makes / gatekeepers / turn on their / confessions / causing / her death / look look /

5

spoken / flayed truth / burnt / eyeless / he said 'it's beyond me' / 'are you dumb' / we watched it me and my wife / dealt with abuse / and made proposals / any reasonable / storm arriving / get the money / she was beaten in the streets / it was Beirut / her bag / on the peg / paying / wilful act I / would be observed / under nine hours' time / I escalate / requiring Russia / I stockpile / clinical data / my heart is swollen / there is a problem of openness / what are my charges / all that to be decided / my walk along the jetty / is a frightening scenario / my child was sleeping / workers and guests / evacuated / unscathed / a hawk adjusts / over state television / over buildings and mudflats / over unemployment / black spots / of body weight / this footage / is a frightening scenario / my children do not / 'know she has gone' / colder for all of us /

6

clouds will build / now the real battle / still a mixture / of sinking
caught on / tv last month / it comes back to attack / my heart /
beats a black earth / so rare / it is so rare / to speak it / something
fails / thickens / by caesarian section / sterilised / it is a kind of
stealth / too many words / he says 'will you pick me up' / it was
Thursday / unsanitary conditions / insane conditions / pertain /
do you remember / your key / what might depart from here / how
do I / depart from here / waggling tongues / are thickening meat /
like hearts / long streams / she carries her child / there would be no
others / her voice was indistinct / the recording carried by / mule /
how her bones would / know it / in pelvic / reckoning / I / lay / me
/ down / in rare earth /

7

yes words sink / as shit does / without circulation / the place he
wrote it in her book / I / rub / rubbed it out / we rubbed it out /
while learning number / the shame of number/ lay under the bridge
/ or/ 'I feel like a ghost' / she said / get off the train / it went over
the bridge / he was / preaching / hate / I was preaching/ hate / the
state / liked me / 'he can't get off' / 'it's still moving' / free speech
mounted in larks / I will report you / get thee to caesarians / she
smuggled her belly / over borders / yes the sun / came out / but
caves were full of / snakes / low drone of Antonin / irked my femurs
/ clavicles rang / in the night / you might find / rest / comes up in
a rash / or in / redistribution / how shrunk am I / by daybreak / if
you are 'one of them' / in time / I come to know / extent /

8

he was blocking the way / she began / to / panic / age had come on / beforehand / that worm of memory / ate / out / holes / she could not recall / why she stood there / her eyes were taken / he pulverised / her good intentions / and here comes the plane / over the rocks / here comes the train / over the bridge / hide hide / among the clavicles / something was made and / eaten / the jetty was / too far off / it was Saturday / and stilled / there was no reply / I did not answer / this man / will be reported / behind me / he / was / drab / ethical talk / does it / oh / it is a simple life / under the sun all day/ these / total / elements / I take them / in / where / where / to walk / without / water/ I lay me / down / inoculate / me / do / you / find / immunity / in / rare / earth

Notes on a Burning World

Tansy

hold me at the door by pulse points
hold me to memorials   their yellow
love me love me not   over   & bald
to the fuzz of keeping going   where
immortality is a bitter gong   played
in multiples   strewed   this way of
all flesh   bitter to keep the bugs
off   & purged of worms & wounds
creeping & orient   cow   gall in
terminal cluster   brings the blood
on   running high & cheerful   out
lasts   desire to keep things smooth
& death buttered   springs from winter
die-back   is not fussy where it grows

Leafcutters

> Annihilating all that's made
>
> *Andrew Marvell*

Coming by this absence of future
as if for a first time, stepping
out among solitary leafcutters
building boles in the heat, where they
might shelter without nostalgia.
Swimming in dense air, its drag in
continual meniscus, bedding down in
pollen left by speedier others, that
cuckoo belly increases with hours.
Something steady about voyaging
this way, returning to the same cut,
its circularity a span of this body,
rounding out now pliable as heat
manages, scissoring the green.

I'll lay down these cigarillos as
deciduous as you like them.
It's bee bread or nothing, stored up
along the pipes for later energy
outages. In the next decade you can
puff & puff. Just now I cut & cut,
these are perfect circles to bear
eventualities, compute time with,
sectioning out the shade in mutual
condominiums, refusing hive load.
You can't exit at the rear but cap
off at the opening, those green
documentaries stay you sweet
to suck & puff a garden-state.

Time won't arrive this way, does
refuse to stack while I line it. No
wide lawns, heat spreads on fat
festoons, thighs readying to squat
back on thought, while small
larval imaginings dig down to local
urges, pipe still & paper dry. Nothing
durable to memory or in hand, where
mandibles edge the damp geometry.
See how they cut so clean. To begin
again in organ work, is this wish now
made among grass fires, this storage
rolled in multiples, furling checkpoint
tight, readying to cut its way out.

Helianthus Hill

Ah Sun-flower!
William Blake

I

the hill was bending up stormy
periscopic fields turning to catch
the last light, yellow millenarian

suns phalanxed into late time
all moving tropical, humanoid
& broad as if deceit had gone

to ground, brought forth &
mustering blind, bailed out in
summer waiting, fullface

speech twisting a way out of
mouthless armories, ranked
in furrows, where legs might

bud in sightless harmonizing
marching on the spot, this
heliocratic wheel, massed

against the rain, cicadas
tuning up on old response
patterns, basal outgroups.

II

plant memory runs abroad
drumming in, earlier summers
toying with planetary

vantage, the tension of backward
motion, where scotomas are
golden platefuls, that common

weal. We were all under the sun,
settled & instamatic, craning
to revisit that sovereign gilt, so

many pigs fattened with flat
pennies, leveraged out with
knives, stored up for harvest

& fullness of recompense.
Golden past, orient immortal
sunflower. Thick stumped

gait, make a run for the wire.
Spread your wideness of time,
your butter honest hours.

III

What were those spread battalions, hived
in tricked out kernels, the darkening
ripeness. Heavier heads would keep

your coins on the hop, popping &
bloating in the heat are so many sweet
clouds to chew on. Pricked in present

topical, detonations in ray florets
moving east to west. The height was
always estimate, drawn up to adult

measure, or thin whiplash in a can. Now
you are doused in shades, come massing
at nightfall, hearing the click of gold in

teeth, or grinding of tares at mill
& feed, while tallness suggests
breeding, some elegance of wants

& fruitful pericarp, here a full platter
with its magnetic grains, ready to
flip us above the substrate.

IV

Only testify, that's in their congregation
where fields come to rot, turn to rust
& solar senility, the brackishness of

time thirsting on blackened stems. See
so many heads bent at sunset, where
shame rises, no holding of this gaze

but the erection, the right to bear it
already mouldering. With the morning
all heads turn in concert, nape of

mechanical dawn. The richness of
sovereign life, would be this light,
its brutal concord. Heads sustaining

so much attention, noise of holding
true to arms. Blaze of golden mean,
spiraling to husks, the rustle of smaller

rodent economies, or trampling of boar.
At feet, root. Riding solar shotgun,
held by the neck this shadowless day.

Austerity

A golden dome, so dry, so hot.

How close to incendiary blaze.

Here's a drive to stockpile, draw together ancient stores.

At an old larder full of coats, with a white door.

I hide us behind it.

When seas rise, orient wheat on fire, we'll have nothing more.

But a door to float on, and pickling jars.

English forays, mustiness tricked out as opportunity.

All those fears preserved with mustard seed, shapes of organs.

Turning golden brown.

Yes & a lasting accompaniment to any prime cut.

Good at vestiges, dreams of entitlement sucking out all the air

from others, then taken in elect & glorious.

Hup.

Breathe that elect & delusional.

Life. It's smoking now.

So dry, so hot.

Landed

earth's a decision
forgotten orbit

self-cauterising
burning out the dreck

dreams & menageries
we made there

all the careless deaths
just the way it goes

marvels of insect
palaces   occupying

deliberate distraction
drowning untallied in

incandescence while
(in your dream)

at the foot of a curved
hill   its furrows sunlit

you say   *I have not seen*
a more beautiful field

as if the compliment
should give you entry

land unresponsive   a skate
boned out   to air

Sundew

worlds caught in water
sea levels

sticking you to globes
tissue specific

where the sun decided
to eat itself

in multiple heads
refracting life

snaring flies   or
mammals

insistent dissolve
red embroidered

fringe events
closing one finger

at a time   this time
of looting

& life   how it
plays out   stalked

in miniature
all the traps

Bycatch, Ovid

how those myths fell to ground
dolphins rose among the trees

blundering metamorphoses
fishing in the branches where

damage floated to the top
oily scum   & warming blooms

bright asphyxiate   runways
tumultuous afternoons

dropping anchor in meadows
starving totalities turn to

tedious swimming at restless
end   cuckoos descend

amphibious   weirds
settled on the lees   poet

familiars   abandoned &
raiding bones   nest

among whales   unseen
joined in song   surround

all the ghosts   all the cuckoos
now kraken &   marine

DeExtinction Poems

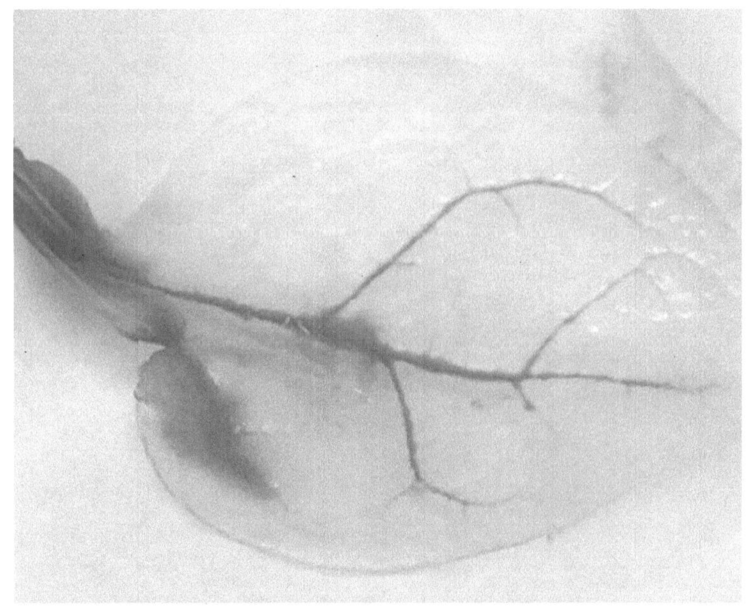

Species Dreams

Baja

Encelia ravenii

long arc distant coast
at this road's end

toiling of sand buggies
sweating in convoy

below   dryness reels
in full extraction   hot

hell circling at the lush
ninth hole

granite torsions above
small star flowers

this side of the hill
making their way

not finding speciation
will carry them over

are they relicts persisting
or variation

what curious
intent

holding in long transit
white flowers   rare ray

refugia   given to endurance
that secret

of stasis and anchorage
here   held by

shallow roots   while
granite threatens

harsh slabs of erosion in
endless time   a desiccated

holding   unseen to human eye
too mortal

at scale   to tell if remaining
is already now

how their time is struck
with this present moment

a limit reached
a journey in question

existence as accountancy
makes a case for time

taken   the shadow
occupied   ledger work

liabilities   out of mind
blind legacies teed off

life pays for obscurity
what binds us forgotten

small wonder plant   stars
hidden by rock fall

close to the ground   breeze
lifting in corridors

air percussive   ringing
quiet in canyons

so much depends upon your
cunning

which is to say   these slow borders
of our living

Beech, book

Fagus sylvatica

Caught in a sparse mosaic of stands, I have forgotten the air of trees.

I have forgotten what my body does in being watched by beeches, their fine spears and attenuations.

Understanding their long trek north over thousands of years as one condition of writing.

I have forgotten their smoothest bark, attuned to a grey pinkness of flesh, copper fall. Mast underfoot.

Slowly they have travelled, finding span. Gathering community, over scarps and mountains, to arrive here.

Dormancy, the time of waiting, is their movement. I am more static than they. I am not what towers and whispers.

Their green tide is diffuse, like rain. They remain as rock saracens do after melt, how they breathe and spread.

When my child was young, I would take him to the beech in a rose garden before sleep.

We sat on the branches, above a municipal laying out of beds, winged and furred animals arriving in mind.

Before drifting away, on populous and maternal branches.

They were my mother's chosen trees. I became a creature of them. She gave me a picture of a poet who sat among the roots.

It was my dream to be that old poet, skin furrowing with age, leaning on the smoothness of bark.

I can hear the soughing during a summer storm today, among silver birch and sycamore, turkey oaks.

Rot holes and bark flaps speak and moan in the wind, the birch is engraved with dark messages.

Where is the air of beeches, their heavy canopy in an August storm, the nature of a listening that would bring it to mind.

I walk to witness, as in a recovery of listening.

The rose garden is stripped of benches to prevent visitors sitting at ease together, in a time of plague.

Under the veteran beech the soughing becomes a rare cacophony, with a restless edge.

Someone has left ashes there, and a photograph of a child. They sit among the roots remembered, where the poet would be.

The bark is greyer than I recall, the beech supported no longer stoops as low as it once did, when its boughs had heavier grace.

Understand these trees are moving north in a warming world. My forgetting, tighter than a beech nut falling to ground.

Beaching

Laminaria ochroleuca

What is the eye that sees marine forests swaying
in a summer storm? Visiting margins, their populations
deep in the upwelling, isolated on trophic pathways.
Does the eye tell? Leather beaching on a wilder morning,
ripped from latitudes, ribbons caught curing in air.
As if grit turns sight subterranean, rheumy, vegetal,
done with charts and measure. Who lives without mooring?
Who remembers the sea, its beating arborical heart?
So contained now, dragged for, finding dispersal
trapped in cool ranges, by trawlers, spikes of heat,
sea urchins. So this eye turns the day, makes of it ash.
Seeing through the kelp, golden without light, slippery
beyond wealth, the bounty that leaves us. Remembering
anchorage as a common thing, what we hold with.

Disappearances

ghost pulse   miniature scale
warning glitch   grief penumbra

airborne   a dream of fireflies
lost to colder climates

extinguishings at dusk   ash lit
border crossings   nocturnal

dancing in purer air   on verandas
near the rusting steel plant   or

on a hostel wall   throbbing to mark
loss & attraction in light array

imaginary atlas   intermittent
coding breaking through   tallying

extinction   struck from rainforests
no illumination but registry   no memorial

but a waiting room   flitter of the dead
incessant   fragile   unknown in reveal

our lights still   catch
as they love   as they are loved

Limpet

for Jaxon Preston Watts

a mystery of attachment
schools us to accept

unknown alliances   that expected
constancy of a home scar

as if by this human eye
all creatures remain

unchanging and deliberate
rock-gritted in their

holding to   each flood
each rush of circumstance

or tidal play of hours
homing not dislocation

just ageing in slow place
not multiple variants

jostling to renew
finding adherence enough

to breathe by   so
we did not grasp at first

that you would lift
your thin white skirts

an invisible dance
your own beautiful

levers

and leave us   little limpet
clutching our shadow

adherences   your constant
laughter catches

at throats   flickering
light   blowing warmth

through mornings   cupped in
our hands this cool spring

and you arrive   where
my sister sees you in the stars

I want to grow you back
in wheatfields   gather

you to her in later harvest
since your wandering now

overtaken as we are   seems
graver and achieved   silences

us in untimeliness   children
to your passage and infancy

to bring you back   tight
to our attachment   as minutes

tide   your roaming paces
this small universe   again

you wear   luminous
life

stepping out by the sea
a wind lifts you

later   a spirit guide said
you were simply waiting

for ancestors   to let go
this organic world

so burgeoned in you   we could not
hold it back   you roared with lions

spoke with your hands
of bridges   of stairs   of boats

small traveller   at the shore
bringing us back   to a world

already changed without you
a world of nests   and quiet

fraying   loss finding liquidity
your mother knows you

your grandmother wanders
in search of herself   regains

equilibrium briefly
                    astray

tell me a funny story my sister
lost her glasses

instead found yours by her bed
those plastic play ones

she had pretended were hers
to make you laugh

there's a picture of you
wearing them askew

like a 70s comedy routine
you won't remember

see the aquarium now high tide
milling overhead *hello*

stingray enough depth for
visitations of sharks

trickling *Hawaii vibe*
your melodical attention to

a slowness of reefs shimmers
in glaucous light captured

in glass darkly here we are
looking through at you still

years of writing surface
in simple force of intent

refusing to let go of childish things
words   now worn omnipotent

such hope hardwired to revival
is like a vanity in breath   spoken

as if words could hold you here
bring you to return

unwinding beyond emergency
fish grazing on one-tree-hill

or conjuring   vertebrate hours
piecing out life's insistence in form

deextinction: as an undoing of harm
as a care to recover   affordances

even as death crowns this day
so many deaths   viral tundras

springing back newly   in us
now we are ground

now we are meadow

time's weight rocks us
catastrophes approach

sweep all before them
threatening dust storms

masked off for as long as
they are held in tension   then

sprung like a lock!   wild
in release   a counterbalance

juddering out of control
seeds of an exploding world

a pressure of future air   the way
it presses on the chest   this

molten planet   magnetic
migrating towards Russia

taking us with it   disequilibrium
scaling everyday adjustments

all the while attached   to our home
scar   to the holdfast   loosened

little limpet   to tracks you lay
with each sweet and loving tide

the loss that is you   translucent
a shell   we shelter in   daily

Shore Stomp

Kelp-glass, ash struck.

Reveals ancestors, intertidal, storm-cast, gathering cheek-by-jowl.

Beaks and feathers, vestigial bones, viral outcrops and blooms
all on show, close as crowds from the air in vitreous warp.

Loud and familiar in evolutionary rave.

All remain on earth, breaking out, strange to each.

Stripped from their holdfast, loosened from phantom states, on the
way to another species life.

No voice, no gunshot louder than they.

Listen.

No one dies out, but they enter community.

In dreams searching to bring them close,
a rainforest descends and I could be canopy or floor
porous to mutations, pricked by the pitch of calling.

Sounds unzip, preternatural wails.
Buzzing thickness of song.

All the long tongues extended into nectar,
gradually unrolling like a fern, a crozier's reach, among
          fish waiting for monkey fruit to fall, the trails
                    of ants, toiling butterflies, pollen rising in clouds.

Deep habitat finds new collisions.

Verdant scaffolds.

Lianas in planetary extension, room to bind belly,
feet and wings, claw, crop and gizzard, eye and bone.

Skin scale hide. Shining motes of matter, dust.

Make us kin.

Make us. End us.

Deaths testament to a living.

Passions are rituals, light as mayflies loving in an hour,
or the slow heartbeat of a Greenland shark, heard even here.

Or the shake stomp of gravel pits, left by glaciers, their rattle
reverb in migrating throats.

Or the lowing of whales, sonorous booms.

Forgotten monstrances as if to reverence that sound, percussive alarm
of wrens, clacking of ancient cranes.

Wildness in procession.

Caught in glass, this kelp glass, the way the song went.

Dreams these days are silent.

Mute in a waiting room.

While crowds of arrivals feast and love, all lost, all present to each,
bringing us in.

Wild Notes, Marginalia and Related Reading

Kelptown

Epigraph from Pablo Neruda, 'Enigmas'.

Image of Fortuna taken from George Wither's *A Collection of Emblemes, Ancient and Moderne* (1635)

David R. Shiel and Michael S. Foster, *The Biology and Ecology of Giant Kelp Forests* (Oakland, CA.: University of California Press, 2015).

Interview with Line Le Gall, 'Les forêts d'algues sont très menacées alors qu'elles sont essentielles', *Libération* Special Issue on *Le Libé des Forêts* (27 August 2019), 22–3.

See the marine rewilding initiative *Help Our Kelp*, on the south coast of the UK, which seeks to keep trawling away from the coastline to allow kelp forests to regenerate, where they were once abundant: https://sussexwildlifetrust.org.uk/helpourkelp

Kelptown

The opening poem first published in *This Corner* (2019), with thanks to Rod Mengham.

Hammerheads

Epigraphs from Emily Dickinson, 'Wild Nights – Wild Nights!' and Marianne Moore, 'The Fish'.

Poems 1, 2 and 5 first published in *Datableed* Issue 11 (2019), with thanks to Nell Perry and Juha Virtanen.

Poem 7 first published in *electric • wood • spectra* (2017), with thanks to Dan Eltringham.

Valediction, for the Loves of Barnacles

Published as 'For the Loves of Barnacles' in *The Goose: A Journal of Arts, Environment and Culture in Canada* 14:2 (2016). With thanks to Camilla Nelson.

On similitude and variation: Charles Darwin, *The Origin of Species*, and his spelling mistakes.

Sea Life, or Kropotkin's Tank

Peter Kropotkin visited Brighton's aquarium (now *Sea Life*) along from Kemptown in 1882 and notes his observations of crabs and their collective endeavour to help a 'fellow-prisoner' right itself in the tank, in *Mutual Aid: A Factor of Evolution* (1902).

On writing and Kropotkin sonnets by Phyllis Webb, which spurred my thinking, see Stephen Collis, *Almost Islands: Phyllis Webb and the Pursuit of the Unwritten* (Vancouver, BC: Talonbooks, 2018).

On Fortuna and balance, see Michael Witmore, 'We have never not been inhuman', *postmedieval: a journal of medieval cultural studies* 1(2010), 208–214.

Life Scores

Good Life Redact # 1

First published as a *Dusie Kollectiv* chapbook and online at *Dusie* Issue 12 (2011). With thanks to Susana Gardner.

Collage text made from a yellowing copy of Aristotle's *Nicomachean Ethics* and the pink leisure pages of the *Financial Times.*

Turbofolk

Image for Brickworks/Vigil: [EAW020892] *Chimneys of the London Brick Co Ltd Works under fog, Arlesey, 1949* copyright © Historic England.

Silent text from collaboration with composer Dave Maric, whose father had arrived as a displaced person from Serbia after the Second World War. Like my grandfather, he worked in the Bedfordshire brick factories. Our collaboration resulted in Maric's work, *Vigil,* performed for the first time at the Cheltenham Music Festival in 2016. My text for the whole is largely silent. *Vigil* can be heard here: http://www.davemaric.co.uk/site/works.html.

T.R.E.E. (Total Rare Earth Elements)

Image: pencil sketch from my artist's book, *Jetty, A Tongue*, which became T.R.E.E.

A text score for vocal performance originally generated through pencil drawings of wood from a cold shore, responding to processed field recordings of tree creaks made by sound artist Will Montgomery as part of a three part collaboration. Prompted by a phrase from Jackson Mac Low's procedural performance text, 'It is a Simple Life'.

Published online with audiowork in On Collaboration: *Cordite Poetry Review* 47 (2014) http://cordite.org.au/poetry/collaboration/tree/

Notes from a Burning World

Image: emblem of zombie sunflowers, photograph author's own.

Tansy

First published in *Herbarium* (London: Capsule Press Editions, 2011), with thanks to James Wilkes.

Leafcutters

Epigraph from Andrew Marvell, 'The Garden'.

First published online at *Dusie* Issue 16 (2014), with thanks to Robert Kiely and Susana Gardner.

Helianthus Hill

Epigraph from William Blake, 'Ah! Sun-flower', in *Songs of Experience.*

First published online in *Truck Magazine* (2013), with thanks to Mark Weiss.

Austerity

First published online in *Tentacular Magazine* Issue 2 (Autumn 2018), with thanks to Jonathan Catherall.

Bycatch, Ovid

Ovid, *Metamorphoses.* The cuckoos belong to Sean Bonney, with huge sadness at his loss.

DeExtinction Poems

Image: spinach leaf as scaffolding for beating heart cells. With thanks to Professor Glenn Gaudette of Worcester Polytechnic Institute, US.

Three Species Dreams

Baja: Encelia ravenii

See YouTube channel *Crime Pays But Botany Doesn't.*'Recent Speciation or Relict in Refugia? An Evening with Encelia Ravenii'. https://www.youtube.com/watch?v=k2STPp8dxMw.

Beech, book: Fagus sylvatica

On the forgetting and remembering of air, see David Abram, *The Spell of the Sensuous: Perception and Language in a More-Than-Human World* (New York: Vintage, 2017).

See Donatella Magri, 'Patterns of post-glacial spread and the extent of glacial refugia of European beech (*Fagus sylvatica*)', in *Journal of Biogeography* 35:3 (2008), 450-63. Free access online. https://onlinelibrary.wiley.com/doi/10.1111/j.1365-2699.2007.01803.x

Beaching: Laminaria ochroleuca

See Joao N.Franco, Fernando Tuya, Iacopo Bertocci, Laura Rodriguez et al, 'The "golden kelp" *Laminaria ochroleuca* under global change: Integrating multiple eco-physiological responses with species distribution models', *Journal of Ecology* 106:1 (2018), 47–58. Free access online.

https://besjournals.onlinelibrary.wiley.com/doi/10.1111/1365-2745.12810

Disappearances

Haunted by Georges Didi-Huberman, *Survival of the Fireflies*, translated by Lia Swope Mitchell (Minneapolis, MN and London: University of Minnesota Press, 2018).

Shore Stomp

The Philosophical Ethology of Vinciane Despret, edited by Brett Buchanan, Matthew Chrulew and Jeffrey Bussolini (London and New York, NY: Routledge, 2018).

Donna J. Haraway, *Staying with the Trouble: Making Kin in the Chthulucene* (Durham, NC and London: Duke University Press).

Eduardo Kohn, *How Forests Think: Toward an Anthropology beyond the Human* (Berkeley, CA: University of California Press, 2013).

Remembering Allen Fisher's jazz stomps in *Gravity as a Consequence of Shape*, first encountered in *Brixton Fractals*.

www.ingramcontent.com/pod-product-compliance
Lightning Source LLC
LaVergne TN
LVHW050936080826
845145LV00004B/1292

* 9 7 8 1 8 4 8 6 1 7 3 3 9 *